Heavenly Seduction

Jennifer Sinclair

Heavenly Seduction
& other poems

Heavenly Seduction & other poems
ISBN 978 1 76041 575 4
Copyright © text Jennifer Sinclair 2018
Cover photo: Jennifer Sinclair

First published 2018 by
GINNINDERRA PRESS
PO Box 3461 Port Adelaide 5015 Australia
www.ginninderrapress.com.au

Contents

Heavenly Seduction 9
   Heavenly seduction 11
   Driftwood 12
   Eros Awakening 13
   Still time 14
   Summer Memories 15
   Ride the Wind 16
   Mermaid 17
   Tide 18
   Port Elliot Dreaming 19
   Silver Sands 20
   Alchemy 21
   The Edge 22
   Sanctuary 23
   Surrender 1 24
   Surrender 2 25
   Surrender 3 26

Bliss 27
   Bliss 29
   The Fragrance 30
   Name 31
   Kiss 32
   Ripe 33
   Juicy 34
   Urgent Embrace 35
   Red Velvet 36
   Blood Rite 37
   Grail 38
   Ecstasy 39
   Gordian Knot 40

Coral	41
Awake	42
Luminous Blue	43
Messenger	44
Caravaggio's angel	45

Falling from Grace — 47

Falling from Grace	49
Lies 1	50
Lies 2	51
Lies 3	52
Lies 4	53
Reckless Faith	54
Angel Belzebuth	55
Watching	56
Anger	57
Womb	58
Mirror Image	59
On Love and War	60
Noise	61
Smile	62
Museum World	63
New Groove	64
Her	65
Shadow Life	66
Almost Blue	67
This love	68
Don't Go	69
Summer without you	70
Smitten	71
Time Stands Still	72
She	73

Redemption — 75

- Redemption — 77
- Apology — 78
- Here… Now — 79
- Saviour — 80
- Prophet — 81
- Beloved — 82
- Landing — 83
- Precious Life — 84
- Cycle — 85
- Heat — 86
- Nearly there — 87
- The Editor — 88
- Poem from the sea — 89
- No Shame — 90
- The Crozier — 91
- Destination — 92
- Closing time — 93
- Waking — 94

Tipping Point — 95

- Tipping Point — 97
- Forgiven — 98
- Cycles — 99
- Mount Ainslie dreaming — 100
- Autumn Afternoon — 101
- Cocoon — 102
- Offering — 103
- Second Coming — 104
- Creation Angel — 105
- Quantum Bond — 106
- Tattoo — 107

Secret	108
New Dawn	109
Quantum Leap	110
Transcendence	111
Peace Pilgrimage	112
Breath	113
Perfect	114
Heaven Within	115
Quest	116

Heavenly Seduction

Heavenly seduction

Love draws you to me,
like the pull of a luminous moon,
an irresistible force
seducing the tide to rise from its ocean bed
and join the celestial body in heavenly union.

Driftwood

I found you by chance
like a piece of driftwood
buffeted and bleached
an unexpected gift, a weary traveller
seemingly abandoned
carried by strong seas, origin unknown
destination a mystery.

Though gnarled and twisted by unforgiving elements
the protective exterior of your birth worn away
closer inspection reveals a time worn surface
the texture of silk.

Eros Awakening

The salty sea washed over me
and desire, like the crest of a wave
rose to meet the heat of a midday sun
responding to its ancient primal call
the lover's name, awakening Eros
from the slumber of the fall.

Still time

Waiting on the station
at the crossroads of duty and freedom
the click clack of the track
the tick tock as the clock counts down
the 10.15 to town
but there's still time for you to pass
for you to see me, waiting
for you to stop, to smile and say
'Going my way?'
and today will be the day I jump into your car
and take the hard right
to freedom.

Summer Memories

Sunlight filtering through vine leaves,
ripe fruit eaten from the tree,
cool lino under warm feet,
sauce bubbling in the kitchen,
lemonade in patterned glasses,
a hiding spot in tall branches,
afternoon shadows across freshly mown lawn,
full tummies, crisp cotton sheets
drifting into dreams.

Ride the Wind

If I could ride the wild wind
and catch the end of his coat,
would he bring me,
golden straw tousled hair,
eyes blue bright a starry night,
cheeks flushed pink as berries bright,
to you.

Mermaid

Descending into this silky jade jewel of ocean
seaweed hair streaming
mermaid memories seeming
almost real,
scaled skin glistening, as I continue listening,
to muffled surf pounding, sounding,
a faint alert,
a gentle voice calling, as I continue falling
to you.

Tide

Moonlight shines over dark water,
a silken veil, gracing a rising tide,
quenching thirsty shores
while footprints made with joyous intent
under a summer sun
disappear into the mysterious depths
of a black ocean.

Port Elliot Dreaming

Frosted sea of blue green grey
turning north around the bay,
blending into cloudy sky,
no longer do I wonder why
sea and sky are joined as one,
making love beneath the sun
like lovers knowing deep within,
where one heart ends and one begins.

Silver Sands

I am bathed in the blue of your sky
as the ocean caresses the shore
with fingers of foam.
I lie upon the sand warmed by the sun
and the song that draws you even deeper
into my heart.

Alchemy

Like Jesus at the marriage of Cana
you changed my water into wine,
and holding the chalice to my lips
bade me drink the sweet dark liquid
until my soul became drunk on love, on life
and the alchemy had begun.

The Edge

Like living out of time in some strange parody of life
like walking in a dream where I can't quite reach you
like knowing that you know but you can't quite tell me
like standing on the edge waiting to fly.

Sanctuary

You are my sanctuary, my sacred space,
like a moth to light I am seduced,
venturing closer to the flame that penetrates the darkness,
returning Heaven to earth.

Surrender 1

Love I surrender,
penetrate this space in me
consume me
deliver me from the pain of separation,
flow through me from your secret source,
fill me up,
make me whole,
you are the teacher, the saviour
do what you will
do what you must
for love is the Law.

Surrender 2

This longing for the other
This sweet surrender
This bitter resistance
Dissolving.

Surrender 3

The memory was a gift,
your sweet soul surrendered its secrets
and my eyes twinkled like stars
in a night-blue velvet sky.

Bliss

Bliss

Wavering between ignorance, and bliss
a solution so simple, but overlooked
in the quest for a crude perfection
man-made in ignorance, while bliss
the liberator, the eternal mystery
reveals the key to the great cosmic puzzle
in the petals of a rose.

The Fragrance

The fragrance evokes more than an image of you,
it penetrates the crisp veneer of polite reality
reaching the molten core
where I am powerless to resist.

Name

Having left your mouth
my name sat lightly on your lips
awaiting the expression
that would breathe me into life.

Kiss

I painted my lips
the colour of plums
enticing you to taste me.

Ripe

Plump persimmon,
red ripe, tight
pregnant with promise,
an explosion of sweet languid flesh
on expectant tongue tips.

Juicy

I am juicy
sun-ripened
sweet
natural
organic
biodynamic
Gaia's gift
blushing pink
peach perfect.

Urgent Embrace

Urgent embrace
I tremble
no going back.

Red Velvet

You graced my body
like a red velvet river
seeking its course
finding the source
of love.

Blood Rite

Like a red slash
on white snow,
slowly melting
beneath you.

Grail

I am the cup,
you filled me
sacred and profane,
and God made meaning,
or was it only me.

Ecstasy

Ecstasy coils around my body
like copper wire, fashioned into form,
tension,
the point before the seed sprouts,
the waters break
and life resolves itself to live,
joyously abandoned
in my ripeness.

Gordian Knot

He tied me round with a Gordian knot
not even Alexander could slice,
and the rise and fall of his sword
was a tenuous hold on power
driven by the old assumptions
of blood and earth.

And unafraid he picked me ripe
revealing my perfect pentagram,
following the footsteps
of Ishtar and Aphrodite.

The serpent saves
in the garden of bliss
and Venus is immortal.

Coral

Spores take flight
and greet the moonlit night
dancing with delight.

Awake

Wide awake
I watch you from the balcony
sleeping.

Luminous Blue

I wear you like a jewel,
luminous blue,
gracing the curve of my celestial body,
a liquid veil
that moves to the tune of a lunar score
in a heavenly duet.

Messenger

You are the source, the experience
the language to be learned
the great song, waiting to be sung
the messenger
existing within the other
separate, yet the same.

Caravaggio's angel

The day is complete,
late afternoon shadows
lengthen across the little kitchen,

The red vase,
the bowl of ripe plums,
summer's scent of roses in full bloom.

She lights the lamp, face flushed radiant,
hair grown longer, glimmers gold
in the lamp's flicker.

She wears the blue dress.

Caravaggio's angel sits by the open French doors
cradling the guitar.
a tangled fall of dark curls, tumbles to his shoulders.

She slices the fruit…he watches.

Music escapes his fingers, dancing across the room,
holding them in an embrace,
somewhere way beyond their ordinary lives.

It's so pure it hurts.

Now the moon is full,
the tide rises in longing response,
he looks up, dark earth eyes capture hers, as blue as the ocean.

And words are inadequate.

Falling from Grace

Falling from Grace

An exile from redemption
you tempted me with elegant deception
and that which would in me become
was temporarily captured, blinded by intrigue.

You, an angel, fallen from grace
a lethal weapon in the wrong hands
creeping through my night dreams
catching me off-guard.

A predator in search of prey
dark stranger bearing gifts
luring me with bits of blue
into the house of sticks.

And me the willing prey
making pretty the grotesque
drawn by the undertow to the very edge
unaware that the door had always been unlocked.

Lies 1

Half of you lies pale
on sheets
crumpled from the game

half of you
lies
darkly crumpled
on pale sheets.

Lies 2

She lies again
he can tell
the way her lips curl
the voice pitched just too high.

The words hang between them.
It's a waiting game.
Truth or dare.
He lies again.
She can tell.

Lies 3

Cloaked in secrets
habits of a lifetime
lies flick easily from a tongue
that slithers across flesh,
unaware of the venom
anticipating its release.

Lies 4

Believing you was too easy,
like falling head first into the still smooth depths
of your words.
So when I hit my head on your jagged edged lies
I realised your deception
and changed my perception.

Reckless Faith

Seduced by a reckless faith
exhausted by idolatry
balanced on a knife edge
blinded by greed
get thee behind me Satan.

Angel Belzebuth

Failed magician
dark predator
lurking in preconscious psyches,
waiting.

Malignant magus
ancient sorcerer
secretly opposing the mysteries,
unredeemed.

Fallen angel
Prince of demons
a devil in disguise
deceiving.

Watching

Lips move soundlessly, bodies rise
and fall
pleasure waves over…you
watch from a distance
the screen flickers, bodies speak,
destinies change imperceptibly, you press
pause and find yourself exposed,
a ghost in the machine
reflected in a revolving door
one frame at a time.

Anger

A seductive companion, maintaining the memories
keeping the enemies, firmly on the hook.
A righteous wrath, justifying vengeance
an eye for an eye, a tooth for a tooth
a punishment projected, ego protected
armoured by pain withholding the truth.

Womb

Barren earth, twisted metal
my womb a tomb, a sad silent sentinel
watching over this secret garden
laid waste by the unbelievers.

Stripped naked, close to the bone
burnt beyond recognition
crumbling, returning to earth
and the beginning.

Mirror Image

I turned to face the mirror
you were standing there instead
reflecting my own sadness
didn't notice you were dead.

On Love and War

There's chaos on this battlefield
called love,
I'm uncertain of my strength, shadows lurk…
imagined or real, an exaggeration
of heart or mind.

I'm confused, who is friend,
who is foe
in the twilight, in the fog of love – of war,
deal me a new card, throw me a lifeline
and reel me in.

Noise

Living in a papier mâché world
grasping at straws
papering over the cracks, filling in the gaps
making something from nothing
everything matters, but nothing is real
unconscious inside the noise,
searching for the silence.

Smile

Smile at me wide
look up from the click clack
of your keyboard
come out from behind your
quantifiable outcomes
quicken my soul
not the pace
it's simple really
requires no project plan
no evidence base
the machine is insatiable
but we are replete
I know you're in there somewhere.

Museum World

In this pantheon
dedicated to a reconstructed past
held together with nuts and bolts
and wire mesh
giant heads all mouth
jaws gaping
leer and laugh at the parade
of incredulous small faces
'It's life, Jim, but not as we know it,' or death
reassembled to resemble
what once were warriors.

New Groove

Going over old ground in familiar territory,
trying to understand the attraction
that kept me caught in that well worn track,
like an old record, convincing the needle
that a familiar rut is safer
than a new groove.

Her

It's enough to know that you are happy,
past regrets and future fears forgotten,
your arms around her youthful waist
safe in her distraction
thoughts of the bigger blue lost
in her sea green eyes.
My autumn is your spring…for now.

Shadow Life

Living is dying in the reflection
a shadow life without redemption
seeking the Grail, but chasing you own tail
your dog is a merry-go-round
and happiness is out-of-bounds
it's the rock or a hard place
on Dante's path.

Almost Blue

A game that no one wins
a place that no one stays
a dream that no one dreams
since you have gone away.

A love that wasn't real
a dream that won't come true
you hold her in your arms
and her eyes are almost blue.

This love

This love
abandoned by one
cherished by the other
that neither time
nor distance
nor failing memory
can erase
can soften
or abate
this breadth
this depth
this shadow
lingering at the edge
of despair
this longing
this suffering
this separation
this death
this love.

Don't Go

Time drifts across the space created by your leaving
a lengthening shadow, moved by forces beyond logic
or rational thought.

All things pass but memories,
If thinking makes it so
I'll remember your return…
Don't go.

Summer without you

Purple jacaranda signals summer
warm perfume of jasmine in the air
swollen raindrops slap upon the paving
spring blossoms tangled in my hair.

Walnut sends it roots a little deeper
grass is growing but for where I lay
the soil beneath my body is the reaper
as you return to water and to clay.

Roses bloom and offer up their petals
a single bird above me sings your song
music is the salve that heals this aching
as life still wills me to go on.

None of it is enough without you.

Smitten

I am smitten.
In your absence I have created a graven image
to worship,
I escape into the dream
lay flowers at your feet
light candles in the dark corridors
of the cathedral,
I wander amongst the silent things,
the dust and stones
and fallen idols that litter
the graveyard of failing memories,
there is no pot of gold
at the end of the rainbow
and language holds no consolation
in the agony of separation.

Time Stands Still

Time stands still
my heart is in your hands
winter on the hill
nature understands.

My heart is in your hands
love will find a way
nature understands
as night turns into day.

Love will find a way
as winter turns to spring
as night turns into day
and bells begin to ring.

As winter turns to spring
and blossoms grace the tree
bells begin to ring
and you return to me.

Under blossoms on the tree
I will wait until
you return to me
and time stands still.

She

She gives you a kiss
I give you the sky
she wants you to promise
I want you to fly
she asks for a ring
I want you to sing
her love is a river
my soul is the sea.

Redemption

Redemption

Like a petulant child ignoring the master
I cast the words as stones, but
you looked upon me with such compassion
that your wounds became mine
and feeling your pain, I cast out the demon in my heart,
healing yours.

Apology

The apology came with a sigh
last autumn leaf surrendered.

Here... Now

I don't need to know what you did...back then
or who you thought you were.
I see the man in front of me...here...now
who looks at me and sees a rose.

Saviour

Tortured paths, rusty nails
Forgiving when all else fails.

Prophet

Nailed to the cross of matter
hailed as the prophet
failed or just forgiving?

Beloved

Beloved
you are the star in the heart of matter
the fire of desire
within my circle of infinite experience.

Landing

Touching down on hallowed ground
where others of little faith had crash landed
stepping lightly to avoid the cracks where seeds
might chance to grow
a giant leap for men with feet of clay
a small step for angels.

Precious Life

Precious life
deeply turned
finely tuned
a work in progress
a story half-written
a journey half-travelled
a song
waiting to be sung.

Cycle

Life waits for liberation
tension triggers germination
from grey to green then green to grey
life begins then death decays.

Heat

High on the heat
toes dipped in shallow water
contemplating time and tide
waiting for no one.

Nearly there

The closer I got the nearer I came
the clearer I saw the truth of the game
the deeper I felt the stiller I stood
what no longer served fell away as it should.

The Editor

Fast forwarding a life on pause
skipping the ads
the useless bits of information
the introduction
the indoctrination
seeking a revelation
re-editing the director's cut
creating a *dolce vita*
in the Cinema Paradiso
of my mind
like Betty Blue
waiting for the bolt.

Poem from the sea

When I read your poem from the sea
I recognised the old you, at one with the blue
captivated by her cold beauty
unconcealed by the façade of self
rich with being, pure
filled with wonder, touched
by a moment of truth, that found you
open and spoke to you
in the language of eternity.

No Shame

There is no shame in loving a man
whose heart is big and deep as an ocean.
For shame is death and he is life
rich with being, pure – complete.
Merciful God, let this joy transcend the fear
let bliss illuminate my mind and lead me back
to perfect peace.

The Crozier

I lead him to the hidden glade
protected by the crozier
and bid him touch
the small stone heart
that had been waiting for him there.

And overhead a flawless sky
reflects the blue within my eyes
and blossoms on the wild pear
will make a garland for my hair

and years ago he held my heart
and loved me gently as my man
so now I lead him back to his
as tenderly I take his hand.

So friend
take my hand
and walk upon this sacred land
where perfect peace and purity
and innocence is all we see
and truth and love
will set us free.

Destination

Was it fate
or destiny
weaving
in silent
anticipation
a destination
fixed or mutable.
The balance had shifted perceptibly
and the darkness understood.

Closing time

The last song travels into the night
beyond the pub, the girls,
the last drinks,
the lonely ones who stay to the bitter end.

Remember when we held the world
in just one note,
crisp and pure as an autumn night
before it turns to winter's chill.

Outside a full moon lights up the sky
too vast and beautiful to comprehend.
And the last song is the silence.

Waking

Waking in darkness
stars still inside
dreams
impatient to be remembered
a little bit of magic
and a whole lot of heart
opens every closed thing
till the light streams in.

Tipping Point

Tipping Point

The tipping point was reached one ordinary afternoon
amid the grace of boyish charm.
The finger of fate tipped the last domino
setting off a chain reaction.
A fission, or was it fusion
of star crossed lovers
either way, who can say
how one small heart, touched by a spark
can ignite a whole universe.

Forgiven

Last streak of sun
across a summer-blue sky
softening at the edges
to autumn's first tinge of kindness,
a time-triggered remembering
as each season turns and returns
according to the gift of creation
that power of perfect peace
the sanctity of oneness, the hallowed name
that delivers us from evil
and forgives the fragile force of man.

Cycles

Winter departs
spring returns with a flurry
summer anticipates the ripening of cherries,
autumn is a memory.

Mount Ainslie dreaming

In the clear light above the valley
a snapshot in time
sits framed by the circle of ancient hills
against the blue sky wall of Her gallery
and we embrace
in the warmth of winter coats
against the chill of a Canberra winter
inside a greater truth.

Autumn Afternoon

Autumn afternoon
time stands still
a tapestry of beauty
colours in the hill
captured by this love
my heart is in your hands
what we don't yet know
God understands.

Cocoon

Driving along the coast road
hugging the curve of ancient hills
worn down by time
an old wind whips the windscreen
the engine purrs
somewhere else the world is whipping up a storm
but safe inside this red cocoon
we remember the dance
a slow spiral turning
a coming together
imagining.

Offering

A red-petal rose offering to you
whose love I gather up and store like a harvest for winter.
Seasons turn, roots dig deeper into clay that will one day
claim our bones amongst the seeds and stones
a wild bird sings the blues from its tiny fragile heart
as we unravel for the last time
hold me tight
until the blossoms blossom.

Second Coming

The world is waiting for the great attractor
the second sun rising,
forging a path through chaos,
joining the dots of evolution.
An idea whose time has come, consciousness
nesting in a rosebud…unfolding.

Creation Angel

Reduced to her elemental nature, unrestrained
by the machinations of the moral mind
dark matter enters the sacred space
torn open by nature's power, unrelenting
cosmic passion made manifest in her
turning the inside out, the outside in
returning to the zero point
to ignite the immortal sun.

Quantum Bond

In that single speck of cosmic dust
there was no 'us', no 'me' no 'you'
just one not two
now time and space create a place
where you and me appear to be
two separate bits of energy,
but hidden from the common view, the love of two
reveals a bond, entangled in a quantum world
I think your name and you respond

Tattoo

My skin knew your names
before you were born
when you were single cells
too beautiful to stay hidden
my love was never a quiet whisper
pain was tenderness and penitence
endured for you
each name a link revealed in ink
the body remembers.

Secret

You are a boy, he is a man,
convinced in conventional wisdom.
You whispered in my ear, a secret.

New Dawn

When the world stops turning, and time stands still
when the magic returns, and the miracle happens
when the new day dawns, and the music begins
I will rise inside this love and kiss the sun.

Quantum Leap

Is it possible
a world brought into being
by our conscious observation,
participation of mind and matter
in an alchemy of infinite possibility?

Were we hoodwinked by Newton's law
like actors in a divine play,
unconsciously obeying
a cause and effect world
a linear reality?

They say the end times approach,
an inferno
or 21st century flood.
Or perhaps without effort
one world moves into another.
A quantum leap of awareness
that floods the collective unconscious.

The 100th monkey drops its weapon
raising its eyes skywards to greet the new dawn.
Jung smiles,
what will happen next?

Transcendence

Uprooting my soul from blood and earth and fire
planting it lightly at the edge of that great ocean
of your heart which has been waiting for me,
the journey to the horizon, unreachable, transcendent
is begun.

Peace Pilgrimage

Journeying back into myself, collecting dreams
seeking the enemy, and finding it was me.
A peace pilgrimage, decision not to hate,
returning from yesterday, seeking tomorrow
finding today.

I am the one I have been waiting for.

Breath

I dreamt you rose from that eternal ocean
like a fish out of water
your breath seeking mine, our bodies entwined
carried by the tide,
we ride on waves of dark imagining.

Let others dream of the sun's rays
dark is the lover who liberates my soul
with all of life and death
in that healing breath.

Perfect

You are perfect,
a flower fashioned from love, coloured by light
made visible only in your presence.

Give up the striving to be what you already are,
your nature is not an effort in beauty that needs improving,
it is complete.

You are perfect.

Heaven Within

Give me nothing, no badges of honour, no pretensions,
just the freedom of emptiness,
the slow ebb and flow.

Erase the false exterior, the showy sham, the tacky cladding,
awaken my senses to pure purpose of being,
to now, not once or future,

Let me enter the real,
the pearl of my wisdom, the kingdom of heaven
within.

Quest

It is as it is, singular and perfect,
all possibilities converge,
irrefutable, sublime, numinous.

Stripped of all adornment, creeds, dogmas, ideas.
There are no more questions, the quest has ended,
my heart unfolds…relieved.

www.ingramcontent.com/pod-product-compliance
Lightning Source LLC
Chambersburg PA
CBHW070101120526
44589CB00033B/1414